NARRATIVE THERAPY EXPLAINED

A Comprehensive Guide To Transformative Techniques, Effective Storytelling, And Practical Applications For Personal Growth And Counseling Success

DR. MELISSA STOTLER

Copyright © 2023 by Dr. Melissa Stotler

Disclaimer:

The data in this book, is solely meant to be informative and instructional.

This book is not intended to replace expert medical advice, diagnosis, or care. No medical, health, or other professional services are offered by the author, publisher, or any affiliated parties

Individual outcomes may differ in the practice of these therapies, which entail a variety of approaches and methodologies.

A one-on-one session with a trained or certified healthcare professional is still preferable. It is best to consult a trained healthcare provider before making any decisions regarding your health.

The author of this book is not affiliated with any specific website, product, or organization related to any of these therapies.

All reasonable measures have been taken by the author and publisher to guarantee the authenticity and dependability of the material contained in this book.

Contents

Narrative Therapy Explained offers a comprehensive exploration of the foundational principles and practical applications of narrative therapy. This book delves into the core theories that underpin narrative therapy, highlighting key theorists and their contributions to the field. By examining the concept of the "narrative" and its pivotal role in shaping therapeutic practice, readers gain a deep understanding of how clients' stories influence their therapeutic journeys. The text explores the critical function of language in therapy, emphasizing how the therapeutic relationship is cultivated and sustained throughout the process.

The book meticulously outlines the narrative therapy process, from initial assessment and goal setting to the practical techniques used in deconstructing problems and re-authoring stories. Readers will learn about various methods for identifying and building on clients' strengths, as well as the collaborative approach essential to effective narrative therapy. The section on techniques and tools further enriches the reader's knowledge with practical strategies such as externalizing problems, mapping their influence, and utilizing letters, journals, metaphors, and stories.

Working with different populations is another key focus, with dedicated discussions on narrative therapy for children, adolescents, couples, and families, as well as considerations for diverse cultural backgrounds. Through detailed case studies, the book provides practical examples of narrative therapy in action, showcasing its application across individual, couple, family, and group settings.

The text also addresses common challenges and limitations within the practice, including resistance, ambivalence, and the integration of narrative therapy with other modalities. Ethical considerations are thoroughly examined, ensuring practitioners understand the principles of confidentiality, professional boundaries, and ongoing competence.

Lastly, the book provides valuable resources for further learning, including recommended literature, online resources, training programs, and professional networks. It also looks ahead to future directions in narrative therapy, exploring emerging trends, evidence-based practices, and the integration of technology into therapeutic practice.

CHAPTER ONE

FOUNDATIONS OF NARRATIVE THERAPY

Narrative therapy is a distinct form of psychotherapy that focuses on the stories we construct about our lives. It operates on the premise that our identities and experiences are shaped by the narratives we tell ourselves and others. This approach emphasizes the idea that people are not defined by their problems but by their stories, which can be re-authored to foster a sense of empowerment and new possibilities.

At its core, narrative therapy is collaborative and respectful, involving both the therapist and the client in the process of exploring and reshaping the client's life story. The therapy is grounded in the belief that people are the experts on their own lives and that they can change their stories to align with their values and aspirations. By working with clients to deconstruct unhelpful narratives and reconstruct more positive ones, narrative therapy aims to help individuals develop a stronger sense of self and agency.

Key Theorists And Influencers

Several key theorists have significantly contributed to the development of narrative therapy. Michael White and David Epston are among the most prominent figures in this field. White, a psychologist from Australia, is known for his work on the role of stories in shaping identity and his development of the therapeutic techniques used in narrative therapy. His collaboration with Epston, a family therapist from New Zealand, led to the formulation of many core concepts in narrative therapy.

David Epston has also made substantial contributions, particularly in applying narrative therapy to family therapy.

Together, White and Epston wrote several influential books and articles that have shaped the practice and understanding of narrative therapy.

Their work emphasizes the importance of externalizing problems and re-authoring life stories, which are central to the narrative therapy approach.

The Concept Of The "Narrative"

The concept of the "narrative" in narrative therapy refers to the stories we create about our lives.

These narratives help us make sense of our experiences and shape our identities. According to narrative therapy, these stories are not fixed but are dynamic and can be altered. The way we interpret our experiences and the stories we tell ourselves about those experiences play a crucial role in shaping our emotional and psychological well-being.

Narrative therapy focuses on exploring these personal narratives to understand how they influence our behavior and emotions.

By examining and challenging these narratives, clients can gain new perspectives and develop healthier ways of understanding themselves and their situations.

This process often involves identifying and questioning the underlying assumptions and beliefs that inform a person's narrative and working to develop alternative, more empowering stories.

Understanding The Client's Story

In narrative therapy, understanding the client's story is fundamental. The therapist's role is to listen carefully to the client's account of their life and experiences, without imposing their own interpretations. This involves exploring the client's background, values, and the context in which their current problems have developed.

By giving the client the space to narrate their story, the therapist helps them uncover the meanings and beliefs that shape their current struggles. This process is collaborative, with the therapist and client working together to understand how the client's narrative has influenced their behavior and emotions. The goal is to identify and challenge problematic narratives and work towards constructing new, more positive ones that align with the client's values and goals.

The Role Of Language In Therapy

Language plays a crucial role in narrative therapy. The way we use language shapes our understanding of ourselves and our experiences. In narrative therapy, language is not just a tool for communication but a powerful force in constructing and deconstructing personal narratives.

Therapists use language to help clients externalize their problems, which means viewing problems as separate from themselves rather than defining their identity by the problem. For example, instead of saying "I am anxious," a client might say, "I am struggling with anxiety." This shift in language helps to reduce the problem's power over the client's identity and opens up possibilities for change.

Therapists also use language to facilitate the re-authoring of the client's story. By guiding clients to use language that reflects their values and desired outcomes, therapists help them create new narratives that support their well-being. This process often involves exploring the ways in which language has been used to reinforce negative stories and finding alternative ways to express and understand the client's experiences.

Exploring The Therapeutic Relationship

The therapeutic relationship in narrative therapy is characterized by collaboration and respect. Unlike more traditional therapeutic approaches where the therapist might take a more authoritative stance, narrative therapy emphasizes a partnership between the therapist and the client. This relationship is based on mutual respect and a shared commitment to exploring and reshaping the client's narrative.

In this collaborative process, the therapist acts as a facilitator rather than an expert. They work with the client to explore their story, challenge unhelpful narratives, and develop new ways of understanding and approaching their issues. This partnership helps to empower clients, giving them a sense of ownership over their therapy and their personal growth.

The therapeutic relationship also involves validating the client's experiences and acknowledging their expertise about their own life. By creating a safe and supportive environment, the therapist helps the client feel valued and understood, which is crucial for effective narrative work and personal transformation.

CHAPTER TWO

THE NARRATIVE THERAPY PROCESS

Initial Assessment And Goal Setting

The narrative therapy process begins with an initial assessment and goal setting. This crucial first step involves understanding the client's story and identifying their challenges.

During this phase, the therapist engages in open dialogue to explore the client's experiences, beliefs, and the contexts in which their problems arise.

It's essential for the therapist to listen actively and empathetically to grasp the nuances of the client's narrative.

Goal setting is a collaborative effort where the therapist and client work together to define what success looks like for the client. This involves setting clear, realistic, and achievable goals based on the client's values and aspirations. For example, if a client feels overwhelmed by stress at work, the goals might include developing healthier work-life boundaries and building resilience strategies. The aim is to create a roadmap that guides the therapy process and provides a sense of direction and purpose.

Techniques For Deconstructing Problems

Deconstructing problems is a key technique in narrative therapy. This process involves breaking down the client's issues into smaller, more manageable parts to better understand their origins and impacts.

The therapist helps the client to examine how societal, cultural, or familial narratives have shaped their understanding of the problem.

For instance, if a client struggles with self-esteem issues, deconstruction might involve exploring how societal expectations and personal experiences have contributed to their self-perception.

By questioning and analyzing these influences, clients can gain insights into how these narratives have constructed their problem and begin to view it from a different perspective. This helps in reducing the problem's power and opens up possibilities for change.

Re-Authoring And Reframing Stories

Re-authoring and reframing are central techniques in narrative therapy that focus on reshaping the client's personal narrative.

Re-authoring involves helping the client to rewrite their story in a way that reflects their values, strengths, and preferred outcomes.

This process encourages clients to envision a new, more empowering narrative that aligns with their true selves.

Reframing complements re-authoring by changing the way clients interpret their experiences.

It involves presenting the client's story from a different angle, highlighting their resilience and resourcefulness rather than focusing solely on problems.

For example, if a client has faced repeated failures, reframing might involve viewing these experiences as learning opportunities and steps toward personal growth.

This shift in perspective can enhance self-efficacy and promote positive change.

Identifying And Building Strengths

Identifying and building strengths is another crucial aspect of narrative therapy. The therapist collaborates with the client to uncover their inherent strengths and resources that can be leveraged to overcome challenges.

This involves exploring past successes, skills, and qualities that have helped the client navigate difficult situations.

For example, if a client has experienced job loss, identifying their strengths might involve recognizing their adaptability, problem-solving abilities, and support networks.

By focusing on these strengths, the therapist helps the client to build confidence and develop a sense of agency. This approach shifts the focus from what is wrong to what is possible, fostering a more optimistic outlook and facilitating progress.

Collaborative Approach With Clients

The collaborative approach in narrative therapy emphasizes partnership and mutual respect between the therapist and client.

The therapist views the client as the expert on their own life and works together with them to explore and address their concerns.

This approach fosters a sense of equality and collaboration, making the therapy process more engaging and effective.

In practice, this means involving clients in every step of their therapeutic journey, from setting goals to evaluating progress.

The therapist uses open-ended questions and reflective listening to encourage clients to share their perspectives and insights.

For instance, rather than dictating solutions, the therapist might ask, "What strategies have worked for you in the past?" This collaborative stance empowers clients to take an active role in their therapy, leading to more meaningful and sustainable change.

CHAPTER THREE

TECHNIQUES AND TOOLS IN NARRATIVE THERAPY

Externalizing The Problem

Externalizing the problem is a cornerstone technique in narrative therapy. It involves separating the issue from the person. Instead of saying "I am anxious," you would frame it as "Anxiety is affecting me." This shift in perspective allows individuals to see their problems as separate entities rather than inherent parts of their identity.

By viewing problems as external forces, clients can gain distance from them. This distancing helps reduce self-blame and fosters a more objective view. For instance, if someone struggles with depression, they might refer to it as "the depression" rather than "my depression." This approach encourages individuals to address the problem as an external challenge they can tackle rather than a personal failure.

In practice, externalizing involves discussing the problem as if it were a character with its own motivations and behaviors. This method not only makes the problem seem more manageable but also empowers clients to fight against it collaboratively rather than feeling overwhelmed by it.

Mapping The Influence Of The Problem

Mapping the influence of the problem involves exploring how the issue impacts various aspects of a person's life and how it interacts with their surroundings. This technique helps individuals understand the extent of the problem's reach and its effects on their daily activities, relationships, and self-perception.

To map the influence, clients and therapists might create visual diagrams or charts. These tools illustrate how the problem affects different domains, such as work, family, and personal well-being.

For example, if a client is dealing with anxiety, they might map out how anxiety affects their job performance, relationships, and overall health.

This process helps clients recognize patterns and identify specific areas where the problem exerts its influence. By understanding these dynamics, clients can pinpoint where to apply interventions and develop strategies to reduce the problem's impact.

Mapping also highlights areas where clients have already managed to mitigate the problem's influence, celebrating small victories along the way.

Identifying Alternative Narratives

Identifying alternative narratives involves uncovering and embracing new stories about oneself that contrast with the dominant problem-saturated narrative.

This technique encourages clients to explore different perspectives and possibilities that may have been overshadowed by the problem.

Clients work with therapists to identify and articulate these alternative narratives. For instance, if someone primarily views themselves as a failure due to past mistakes, the therapist might help them reframe this view by exploring instances where they succeeded or overcame challenges. This process allows clients to see themselves through a more positive and nuanced lens.

Creating alternative narratives often involves revisiting past experiences and finding new meanings or strengths within them. These narratives are not just about positive thinking but about recognizing and validating personal resilience and capabilities. This shift helps clients build a more empowering and hopeful view of themselves and their future.

Using Letters And Journals

Letters and journals are practical tools used in narrative therapy to facilitate reflection and self-expression. Writing letters or keeping a journal allows clients to articulate their thoughts, feelings, and experiences in a structured way, offering a different perspective on their situation.

In narrative therapy, clients might write letters to themselves, to the problem, or to significant others.

These letters serve as a means of expressing and clarifying emotions, setting goals, or negotiating changes. For example, a client might write a letter about their anxiety, describing how it affects them and expressing their desire to overcome it.

Journaling provides a space for ongoing reflection. Clients can document their daily experiences, track progress, and explore their evolving narratives.

By regularly writing about their experiences, clients gain insights into their thoughts and behaviors, which helps in recognizing patterns and making informed decisions about their therapeutic journey.

Role Of Metaphors And Stories

Metaphors and stories are powerful tools in narrative therapy that help clients make sense of their experiences and communicate their struggles in creative ways.

Metaphors offer a way to frame problems and solutions through symbolic language, making complex issues more relatable and understandable.

For instance, a client might describe their depression as a "dark cloud" that follows them around.

This metaphor helps illustrate how the depression feels and its impact on their life. Therapists can use these metaphors to guide conversations, helping clients explore and reframe their experiences.

Stories, whether personal or borrowed, serve to illustrate and reinforce new narratives. Clients might use stories to highlight their strengths or envision a future where the problem no longer dominates their lives. Sharing these stories fosters a sense of agency and hope, helping clients see their potential for change and growth.

CHAPTER FOUR

WORKING WITH DIFFERENT POPULATIONS

Narrative Therapy, with its emphasis on stories and personal meaning, can be effectively adapted to a variety of populations. Each group—whether children, adolescents, couples, or families—brings its unique set of needs and dynamics. Understanding how to tailor narrative techniques to fit these diverse contexts can enhance the therapeutic process and support meaningful change.

Narrative Therapy With Children

Creating a Safe Space

When working with children, it's essential to establish a safe and comfortable environment. Children often communicate through play, art, and stories rather than traditional conversation.

Using toys, drawings, or storytelling can help them express their thoughts and feelings more naturally.

Engaging Through Stories

Children are naturally drawn to stories. Therapeutic storytelling can be a powerful tool in this context. By creating or retelling stories that mirror the child's experiences or challenges, therapists can help children understand and reframe their own narratives. For example, a story about a brave character overcoming obstacles can help a child gain confidence in dealing with their own difficulties.

Interactive Techniques

Incorporating interactive methods such as role-playing or puppetry can make therapy more engaging for children. These techniques allow children to explore different perspectives and solutions in a playful and non-threatening way. This approach can be especially effective in helping children articulate their emotions and experiences.

Adapting Techniques For Adolescents

Addressing Developmental Changes

Adolescents are navigating significant developmental changes and may struggle with issues related to identity, autonomy, and peer relationships. Narrative therapy with adolescents often involves exploring their self-concept and the roles they see themselves playing in their personal narratives. Encouraging them to articulate their values, goals, and challenges can provide clarity and direction.

Empowering Through Choice

Empowerment is a key theme in adolescent narrative therapy. Adolescents benefit from having choices in how they tell their stories and in the techniques used during therapy. Providing them with options, such as different methods of expression or topics of focus, can help them feel more in control of their therapeutic process.

Incorporating Technology

Many adolescents are comfortable with technology and digital media. Incorporating these elements—such as creating digital stories or using social media platforms—can be an effective way to engage them in therapy. This approach not only resonates with their everyday experiences but also allows them to explore their narratives in a medium they are familiar with.

Narrative Therapy In Couples Counseling

Identifying Shared Narratives

In couples counseling, narrative therapy focuses on understanding and reshaping the shared narratives that partners have about their relationship. By exploring the stories they tell about each other and their relationship, couples can gain insight into how these narratives shape their interactions and conflicts.

Exploring Relationship Roles

Couples often fall into specific roles or patterns within their relationship narratives. Narrative therapy helps partners identify these roles and understand how they contribute to relationship dynamics. By rewriting their narratives, couples can break out of unproductive patterns and develop healthier ways of relating to each other.

Fostering Collaboration

Encouraging collaborative storytelling is crucial in couples therapy. Each partner's perspective is valued, and both are invited to contribute to a new, shared narrative that reflects their mutual goals and values. This collaborative approach fosters a sense of partnership and mutual understanding.

Applications In Family Therapy

Understanding Family Narratives

In family therapy, narrative therapy helps families examine and reframe their collective stories. By understanding the roles and expectations each family member has, families can address longstanding issues and develop new, more constructive narratives that enhance family cohesion.

Highlighting Strengths and Resources

Families often have existing strengths and resources that may be overlooked. Narrative therapy helps families identify and build on these positive aspects of their stories. This strengths-based approach can empower families to address challenges more effectively and foster resilience.

Facilitating Communication

Improving communication within the family is a key goal of narrative therapy. By exploring and discussing family narratives, family members can gain insight into each other's perspectives and improve their communication. This process helps in resolving conflicts and building stronger, more supportive relationships.

Working With Diverse Cultural Backgrounds

Cultural Sensitivity and Respect

When working with individuals from diverse cultural backgrounds, it is important to approach narrative therapy with cultural sensitivity and respect. Understanding and acknowledging cultural values, beliefs, and practices can enhance the therapeutic relationship and ensure that the therapy is relevant and respectful.

Adapting Techniques to Cultural Contexts

Narrative techniques should be adapted to fit the cultural context of the client. For example, some cultures may place a strong emphasis on family and community narratives, while others may focus more on individual experiences. Tailoring therapeutic techniques to align with these cultural values can make the therapy more effective and meaningful.

Inclusive Storytelling

Inclusive storytelling involves recognizing and integrating the diverse cultural narratives that clients bring into therapy.

By validating and incorporating these cultural narratives, therapists can help clients explore and reshape their stories in a way that honors their cultural identity and experiences. This approach fosters a more inclusive and supportive therapeutic environment.

CHAPTER FIVE

CASE STUDIES AND PRACTICAL APPLICATIONS

Case Study 1: Individual Therapy

In this case study, we explore how narrative therapy was applied to an individual struggling with anxiety and self-doubt. The client, Emma, had been experiencing significant distress related to her perceived lack of career success and personal fulfillment. Through narrative therapy, the goal was to help Emma reframe her life story and shift her perspective on her challenges.

The process began with Emma sharing her story in detail, focusing on the events and experiences that contributed to her feelings of inadequacy. The therapist listened actively, highlighting the dominant narratives that were shaping Emma's self-perception. By identifying these negative narratives, they were able to challenge and reframe them.

Together, they worked on creating a new, more empowering narrative. Emma was encouraged to view her career and personal setbacks as part of a larger, more complex story rather than as defining failures. The therapist helped her identify her strengths, achievements, and the positive aspects of her journey that had previously been overshadowed by negative self-talk.

Emma's progress was marked by a noticeable shift in her self-esteem and outlook on life. She began to see her experiences through a more balanced lens, recognizing her resilience and growth. This case illustrates the power of narrative therapy in helping individuals reconstruct their personal narratives to foster a healthier self-image and greater life satisfaction.

Case Study 2: Couples Therapy

In this scenario, narrative therapy was used with a couple, Alex and Jamie, who were experiencing frequent conflicts and communication issues. Their relationship was marked by ongoing arguments about finances and future goals, which had led to a significant emotional disconnect.

The therapy process involved both partners sharing their individual perspectives and stories about their relationship. The therapist facilitated discussions that uncovered underlying narratives about their roles and expectations within the relationship. It became clear that both Alex and Jamie were operating from conflicting and outdated scripts about their partnership.

The next step was to help them co-create a new narrative for their relationship. The therapist guided them in exploring their shared values and goals, encouraging them to build a joint story that emphasized cooperation and mutual support. They worked on acknowledging and validating each other's experiences and redefining their roles in a way that aligned with their renewed vision for their relationship.

Over time, Alex and Jamie reported improved communication and a deeper understanding of each other's needs and aspirations.

The case demonstrates how narrative therapy can help couples renegotiate their relationship dynamics and develop a more collaborative and harmonious partnership.

Case Study 3: Family Therapy

This case study involves a family dealing with generational conflicts and miscommunications. The Smith family had been struggling with issues related to parenting styles, sibling rivalry, and differing expectations among family members.

In family therapy, the narrative approach begins with each family member sharing their perspectives and personal stories.

The therapist worked to map out the family's overarching narrative and identify patterns of interaction that were contributing to the conflicts.

For example, it was discovered that certain family members were adhering to traditional roles and expectations that no longer fit their current situation.

The therapy focused on deconstructing these traditional narratives and exploring alternative ways of relating to one another. Family members were encouraged to share their hopes and dreams and to listen to each other's stories with empathy.

 They collaboratively developed new narratives that fostered a greater sense of unity and mutual respect.

The Smith family found that by redefining their family story, they were able to address long-standing issues and create a more supportive and understanding environment. This case highlights how narrative therapy can be instrumental in resolving family conflicts and enhancing relational dynamics.

Case Study 4: Group Therapy

In this example, narrative therapy was applied in a group setting with individuals dealing with issues related to low self-esteem and social anxiety. The group consisted of members who felt isolated and struggled with their self-worth, affecting their interactions with others.

The group therapy sessions began with each participant sharing their personal narratives and the impact these stories had on their self-perception and social interactions.

The therapist facilitated discussions that helped members identify common themes and narratives within the group. By highlighting these shared experiences, participants were able to connect with each other on a deeper level.

Through narrative exercises, group members were encouraged to reframe their stories and challenge negative beliefs about themselves. The therapist guided them in creating more empowering and positive narratives that emphasized their strengths and potential.

The group also engaged in mutual support, offering feedback and encouragement to each other.

The outcome of the group therapy was a significant improvement in participants' self-esteem and social confidence. They reported feeling more connected to others and more optimistic about their personal growth. This case demonstrates how narrative therapy can be effectively used in group settings to foster a sense of community and individual empowerment.

Lessons Learned And Key Takeaways

The case studies illustrate several key lessons about the practical applications of narrative therapy:

Reframing Narratives: One of the central techniques in narrative therapy is the ability to reframe personal and relational stories. By changing the way individuals or groups interpret their experiences, they can shift their self-perception and improve their overall well-being.

Empowerment Through Storytelling: Narrative therapy empowers clients by allowing them to take control of their own stories. This process helps them to view their challenges as manageable and to recognize their own agency in shaping their lives.

Collaboration and Validation: In both individual and group settings, narrative therapy emphasizes the importance of collaboration and validation. By listening to and validating each other's experiences, clients can build stronger connections and develop more supportive relationships.

Flexibility Across Contexts: The versatility of narrative therapy is evident in its application across different contexts, including individual, couple, family, and group therapy. Each setting benefits from the approach's focus on personal storytelling and collaborative meaning-making.

These insights underscore the effectiveness of narrative therapy in addressing a wide range of psychological and relational issues, highlighting its adaptability and the profound impact it can have on individuals and groups.

CHAPTER SIX

CHALLENGES AND LIMITATIONS

Common Challenges In Practice

Narrative therapy, while powerful, is not without its challenges in practice. One of the main difficulties therapists may encounter is the need for extensive time and effort to help clients deconstruct and reconstruct their personal narratives. This process can be lengthy and requires a deep level of engagement from both the therapist and the client. Clients might also struggle with articulating their stories, particularly if they have been suppressing their feelings or experiences for a long time. Therapists need to be patient and skilled in creating a safe space where clients feel comfortable sharing their narratives.

Another challenge is the potential for misalignment between the client's story and the therapeutic goals. Sometimes, clients might have narratives that are deeply entrenched and resistant to change, which can make it difficult to move forward in therapy. Therapists must be adept at recognizing when a client's narrative might be preventing progress and gently guide them toward alternative perspectives without dismissing their lived experiences.

Addressing Resistance And Ambivalence

Resistance and ambivalence are common in narrative therapy and can significantly impact the therapeutic process.

Resistance often manifests as a reluctance to explore certain aspects of one's story or a refusal to adopt new perspectives. This resistance can stem from a fear of change or discomfort with confronting painful memories. To address this, therapists need to employ strategies that help clients feel supported and understood. This might involve validating the client's feelings and gradually introducing new ways of thinking that align with the client's values and goals.

Ambivalence, on the other hand, involves mixed feelings about changing one's narrative. Clients might recognize the need for change but simultaneously feel apprehensive about altering their self-concept or the way they interact with others.

Therapists can work with ambivalence by exploring the benefits and drawbacks of maintaining versus changing the current narrative. Encouraging clients to weigh the pros and cons can help them make more informed decisions about their therapy goals.

Limitations Of Narrative Therapy

Despite its strengths, narrative therapy has limitations. One notable limitation is that it might not be suitable for clients who are seeking more immediate, symptom-focused solutions.

Narrative therapy emphasizes long-term changes in self-perception and meaning, which can be a slower process compared to other therapeutic modalities that address specific symptoms more directly.

Additionally, narrative therapy may not address underlying biological or neurological factors contributing to psychological distress.

While it is effective in reshaping personal narratives and exploring meaning, it does not replace the need for medical or pharmacological interventions when these are necessary. Therapists should be aware of when to refer clients to other professionals for a more comprehensive approach to their mental health.

Integrating Narrative Therapy With Other Modalities

Integrating narrative therapy with other therapeutic modalities can enhance its effectiveness. Combining narrative therapy with cognitive-behavioral techniques, for example, can provide a more balanced approach. While narrative therapy focuses on changing the story, cognitive-behavioral therapy (CBT) can address specific cognitive distortions and behavioral patterns. This integration allows for a more holistic approach, addressing both the narrative and the practical aspects of a client's difficulties.

Similarly, integrating narrative therapy with mindfulness practices can help clients stay present and observe their thoughts and feelings without judgment. This combination can be particularly useful for clients who need support in managing their emotional responses while working through their narratives. The key to successful integration is ensuring that the modalities complement each other and are tailored to the client's specific needs.

Overcoming Barriers In Diverse Settings

Implementing narrative therapy across diverse settings presents unique challenges. Cultural differences can affect how clients perceive and engage with their narratives.

Therapists must be culturally competent and sensitive to the diverse backgrounds of their clients, adapting their approach to align with the client's cultural values and beliefs. This might involve incorporating culturally relevant practices or understanding how cultural contexts influence the client's narrative.

In organizational or community settings, narrative therapy might face barriers related to power dynamics and group structures. Addressing these barriers requires a collaborative approach where all voices are heard and valued.

Facilitators should work to create an inclusive environment that respects diverse perspectives and facilitates open dialogue. This ensures that the narrative work remains relevant and effective in varying contexts and settings.

CHAPTER SEVEN

ETHICAL PRINCIPLES IN NARRATIVE THERAPY

Narrative therapy is grounded in a set of ethical principles that guide practitioners in delivering effective and respectful care.

These principles revolve around respect for the client's autonomy, a commitment to social justice, and the recognition of the client's expertise in their own life.

Respect for Autonomy: At the heart of narrative therapy is the belief in the client's right to self-determination.

Practitioners honor the client's ability to make choices and decisions about their own life story.

This means engaging with clients in a way that values their perspectives and encourages them to explore and articulate their own narratives without undue influence.

Commitment to Social Justice: Narrative therapists are committed to addressing power imbalances and social injustices that impact clients' lives.

This involves recognizing and challenging societal norms and structures that may contribute to clients' difficulties, ensuring that therapy is inclusive and equitable.

Recognition of Client Expertise: Narrative therapy operates on the premise that clients are the experts in their own lives.

Therapists collaborate with clients to co-create meaning and find solutions, respecting the client's lived experiences and knowledge as central to the therapeutic process.

Confidentiality And Privacy Issues

Confidentiality is a cornerstone of narrative therapy, ensuring that clients can freely share their stories without fear of unauthorized disclosure.

Importance of Confidentiality: Maintaining confidentiality is crucial for building trust between the therapist and the client.

Clients need to feel secure that their personal information and the details of their narrative will not be disclosed to others without their explicit consent. This trust fosters an open and honest therapeutic relationship, which is essential for effective therapy.

Handling Sensitive Information:

Therapists must handle sensitive information with care. This includes securely storing records, avoiding casual conversations about clients in public or shared spaces, and discussing confidentiality agreements clearly with clients at the outset of therapy.

Legal and Ethical Exceptions: There are specific situations where confidentiality might be breached, such as when there is a risk of harm to the client or others, or when required by law. Therapists must navigate these exceptions carefully, ensuring that clients are informed about the limits of confidentiality and the circumstances under which information might be disclosed.

Professional Boundaries

Maintaining professional boundaries is essential in narrative therapy to ensure a respectful and effective therapeutic relationship.

Defining Boundaries: Professional boundaries refer to the limits that define the therapeutic relationship and ensure that interactions remain appropriate and focused on the client's well-being. This includes maintaining a clear distinction between professional and personal relationships.

Avoiding Dual Relationships:

Therapists should avoid dual relationships where they have multiple roles with a client, such as being both a therapist and a friend. Dual relationships can create conflicts of interest and undermine the therapeutic process.

Maintaining Boundaries:

Boundaries are maintained through consistent and respectful behavior, clear communication about the nature of the therapeutic relationship, and adherence to professional codes of conduct. Regular supervision and self-reflection can help therapists stay aware of their own boundaries and potential issues.

Maintaining Competence And Ongoing Learning

To provide effective therapy, narrative therapists must continuously update their knowledge and skills.

Commitment to Professional Development: Narrative therapists are responsible for staying informed about the latest developments in the field. This involves participating in ongoing education, attending workshops and conferences, and engaging in peer supervision.

Self-Reflection and Supervision: Regular self-reflection helps therapists assess their own practice, identify areas for growth, and address any personal biases that may impact their work. Supervision provides an opportunity to discuss challenging cases, receive feedback, and ensure that therapeutic interventions are appropriate and effective.

Adapting to New Knowledge:

The field of narrative therapy evolves, and therapists must be open to integrating new research and methodologies into their practice. This adaptability ensures that therapy remains relevant and responsive to clients' changing needs.

Navigating Difficult Ethical Dilemmas

Ethical dilemmas in narrative therapy can be complex, requiring careful consideration and balanced decision-making.

Identifying Ethical Dilemmas:

Ethical dilemmas arise when there are conflicting values or principles that make decision-making challenging. Examples include situations where clients' desires conflict with professional guidelines or when managing competing interests.

Approach to Resolution: Therapists should use a structured approach to resolve ethical dilemmas, including reviewing relevant ethical codes, consulting with supervisors or colleagues, and reflecting on the potential impact of different courses of action on the client.

Documentation and Transparency: Documenting ethical decisions and maintaining transparency with clients about the decision-making process can help manage dilemmas effectively. Clear documentation ensures accountability and provides a record of the steps taken to address the issue.

CHAPTER EIGHT

RECOMMENDED BOOKS AND ARTICLES

When delving into Narrative Therapy, starting with foundational literature can be incredibly beneficial. For those new to the field or looking to deepen their understanding, a few key texts provide a comprehensive overview of the theory and practice.

"Narrative Therapy: Theoretical and Practice Perspectives" by David Epston and Michael White is a seminal text that lays the groundwork for understanding the principles of Narrative Therapy. Epston and White, pioneers in the field, offer insights into how stories shape our lives and how narrative practices can facilitate change. This book explores the concepts of externalizing problems and reconstructing identity through narrative.

"Re-authoring Lives: Interviews and Essays" by Michael White is another essential read. It expands on the techniques and practical applications of Narrative Therapy, with real-world examples and interviews. White's work helps illustrate how clients can reshape their personal narratives to overcome difficulties and achieve their goals.

"Narrative Therapy: Making Meaning, Making Lives" by Lynne Harris provides a practical guide to applying Narrative Therapy concepts in clinical settings. This book includes case studies and practical exercises, offering readers tools to implement Narrative Therapy techniques effectively.

For articles, the Journal of Narrative Therapy and Community Work offers a range of peer-reviewed articles that explore current research, case studies, and innovations in Narrative

Therapy. These articles can help you stay updated with the latest developments in the field.

Useful Online Resources And Websites

The internet is a treasure trove of resources for those interested in Narrative Therapy. Here are some valuable online platforms to enhance your learning and practice.

The Narrative Therapy Centre (narrativetherapycentre.com) offers a wealth of resources, including articles, case studies, and training opportunities. The site provides insights into the latest research and developments in Narrative Therapy and features materials suitable for both beginners and seasoned practitioners.

Narrative Practice (narrativepractice.com.au) is another excellent resource. It includes a range of educational materials, such as videos and articles, focused on practical applications of Narrative Therapy. The site also offers a comprehensive list of training opportunities and workshops.

The Dulwich Centre (dulwichcentre.com.au) is a hub for Narrative Therapy resources. It features publications, online courses, and an extensive library of articles and books by leading practitioners in the field. Their blog and newsletter provide ongoing updates and insights into Narrative Therapy practice.

For those seeking community engagement and support, The International Journal of Narrative Therapy and Community Work's website (ijntcw.com) offers access to research articles and practical resources. This journal covers a range of topics related to Narrative Therapy and is an excellent resource for staying informed about the latest advancements and discussions in the field.

Training And Certification Programs

Training and certification are crucial for those seeking to practice Narrative Therapy professionally. Several programs provide in-depth training and official certification, equipping practitioners with the necessary skills and knowledge.

The Dulwich Centre offers a variety of training programs, including workshops, online courses, and advanced certification. Their programs are designed to provide comprehensive training in Narrative Therapy principles and techniques, led by experienced practitioners and educators.

The Narrative Therapy Centre provides certification programs for those looking to specialize in Narrative Therapy. Their courses cover a wide range of topics, from basic techniques to advanced practice, and include both in-person and online options.

The Institute of Narrative Therapy offers structured training and certification programs that focus on practical applications of Narrative Therapy. Their programs are designed to help practitioners integrate Narrative Therapy concepts into their work with clients, with a focus on developing practical skills and theoretical understanding.

Professional Organizations And Networks

Joining professional organizations and networks can provide valuable support and opportunities for growth in the field of Narrative Therapy. These organizations offer access to resources, networking opportunities, and professional development.

The International Narrative Therapy and Community Work Association (INTCW) is a global network that connects practitioners and researchers in Narrative Therapy. Membership provides access to a range of resources, including publications, conferences, and workshops.

The Narrative Therapy Centre also serves as a professional network, offering a membership that includes access to exclusive resources, training opportunities, and a community of practitioners dedicated to Narrative Therapy.

The American Association for Marriage and Family Therapy (AAMFT) includes Narrative Therapy among its therapeutic approaches. Membership in AAMFT provides access to resources, professional development opportunities, and a network of professionals in the field of therapy.

Conferences And Workshops

Attending conferences and workshops can significantly enhance your understanding of Narrative Therapy and provide opportunities to learn from leading experts. Here are some notable events to consider.

The International Narrative Therapy and Community Work Conference is a major event that gathers practitioners, researchers, and educators from around the world. The conference features presentations, workshops, and discussions on the latest developments in Narrative Therapy.

The Dulwich Centre's Annual Training Week offers a series of workshops and seminars led by experienced practitioners. This event provides an opportunity for intensive learning and networking with other professionals in the field.

The Narrative Therapy Summer Institute is an educational event that focuses on advanced Narrative Therapy techniques and applications. It includes workshops and sessions led by prominent figures in the field, offering participants a chance to deepen their knowledge and skills.

These conferences and workshops provide valuable opportunities for learning, networking, and professional development, making them essential for anyone serious about advancing their practice in Narrative Therapy.

CHAPTER NINE

FUTURE DIRECTIONS IN NARRATIVE THERAPY

Emerging Trends And Innovations

Narrative therapy, which focuses on the stories individuals construct about their lives, is evolving rapidly. One significant trend is the increasing integration of cultural considerations into therapeutic practices.

Therapists are now placing greater emphasis on understanding and incorporating clients' cultural backgrounds and identities into their therapy.

This trend reflects a broader move toward more personalized and culturally sensitive approaches to mental health.

Another innovation is the application of narrative therapy principles in non-traditional settings.

For instance, there's growing interest in using narrative techniques within schools to support students facing academic and personal challenges. This trend highlights the versatility of narrative therapy in addressing a wide range of issues beyond the traditional therapeutic setting.

Additionally, there is a rising interest in blending narrative therapy with other therapeutic modalities. This integrative approach allows therapists to combine the strengths of narrative therapy with techniques from cognitive-behavioral therapy (CBT), mindfulness, or other frameworks, offering a more holistic treatment plan tailored to individual needs.

Research And Evidence-Based Practices

The field of narrative therapy is increasingly supported by research and evidence-based practices. Recent studies have highlighted its effectiveness in treating various mental health conditions, including depression, anxiety, and trauma. Research has demonstrated that narrative therapy can lead to significant improvements in clients' self-esteem and overall well-being by helping them reframe their personal stories and challenges.

Evidence also supports the use of narrative therapy in group settings, where individuals can benefit from shared experiences and collective storytelling. This approach has shown promise in fostering a sense of community and mutual support among participants, enhancing the therapeutic process.

Moreover, ongoing research is exploring the effectiveness of narrative therapy in diverse populations, including different age groups and cultural backgrounds.

This evidence base is essential for refining practices and ensuring that narrative therapy remains relevant and effective across various contexts.

Expanding Applications In New Contexts

Narrative therapy is finding new applications in various fields beyond traditional psychotherapy.

In the realm of education, teachers and counselors are adopting narrative techniques to address students' personal and academic struggles.

By encouraging students to tell their own stories, educators can help them build resilience and develop a positive self-identity.

In healthcare, narrative therapy is being used to support patients coping with chronic illnesses or major life changes.

By helping patients construct and understand their illness narratives, therapists can improve their overall quality of life and adherence to treatment plans.

Additionally, narrative therapy is being applied in organizational settings to improve workplace dynamics and employee well-being.

By facilitating storytelling and dialogue within organizations, narrative practices can address issues such as conflict resolution, team building, and leadership development.

Integration With Technology And Digital Platforms

The integration of technology and digital platforms into narrative therapy is opening new avenues for practice. Online platforms and apps are being developed to provide narrative therapy tools and resources to a wider audience. These digital solutions offer flexible and accessible ways for individuals to engage in therapeutic storytelling and reflection.

Teletherapy is another significant advancement, allowing clients to participate in narrative therapy sessions from the comfort of their homes. This mode of therapy has proven to be effective and convenient, particularly for those with limited access to in-person services or those who prefer remote engagement.

Virtual reality (VR) and other immersive technologies are also being explored for their potential to enhance narrative therapy. VR environments can create engaging scenarios that help clients visualize and interact with their personal stories in new and meaningful ways.

The Future Of Narrative Therapy Practice

Looking ahead, the future of narrative therapy practice appears promising and dynamic. As the field continues to evolve, there is an increasing emphasis on personalizing and diversifying therapeutic approaches to meet the unique needs of individuals. The integration of cultural competence, evidence-based practices, and technological innovations will likely drive future developments in narrative therapy.

Therapists are expected to embrace these changes, incorporating new tools and techniques to enhance their practice. By staying abreast of emerging trends and research, practitioners can continue to offer effective and relevant therapeutic interventions that support clients in rewriting and empowering their personal narratives.

As narrative therapy expands into new contexts and integrates with various technologies, it will likely continue to provide valuable insights and solutions for individuals navigating their personal stories and challenges.

www.ingramcontent.com/pod-product-compliance
Lightning Source LLC
Chambersburg PA
CBHW061254250726
48653CB00002B/662